God Makes All Things New

By Patricia and Fredrick McKissack

Illustrated by Ching

Augsburg
MINNEAPOLIS

GOD MAKES ALL THINGS NEW

Copyright © 1993 Augsburg Fortress

Scripture quotations unless otherwise noted are from the New Revised Standard Version of the Bible, copyright © 1989 by the Division of Christian Education of the National Council of Churches of Christ in the United States of America.

ISBN 0-8066-2653-4   LCCN 93-70326

Manufactured in the U.S.A.   AF 9-2653

97   96   95   94   93   2   3   4   5   6   7   8   9   10

To Our Sons

"See, I am making all things new."
—Revelation 21:5

Every day, somewhere in
God's world,

life is beginning . . .

and growing . . .

and changing . . .

and making new life.

Every day, somewhere in
God's world,

life is ending . . .

for the large and small . . .

young and old . . .

strong and weak.

Every minute of every day,

life begins . . .

and ends.

But a day will come when
God makes all things new.

And that is God's promise.

A Note to Parents and Friends of Children

Every day we encounter death in some way—through newspaper stories, on television, in our circle of relatives or friends. Sometimes the death is far removed from us. Other times it is painfully near.

Children also encounter death, and often in our attempts to shelter them from the pain that death can bring, we use language that can be confusing. Children need to know that death is a natural occurrence. They need to understand the finality of it.

Yet our faith speaks of a resurrection. God indeed will make all things new. We are reborn children of God, and we have an eternal hope in God's love through Christ.

As you read this book together, take time to answer the questions your child may have about death. Answer truthfully, but avoid overloading your child with unnecessary information. Do not use euphemisms such as "He has passed away," or "She is sleeping." As adults we can decipher what is meant, but children cannot. Above all, share with your child your belief in God's gracious love and salvation. Although all things will come to an end, God's love does not. We can rely on that promise.